Henry Harris Jessup, Noeme Tabet

Letter forwarded by the American Missionaries of Beyrout, Lebanon, Tripoli, Sidon, etc.

To the Evangelical Native Church of Beyrout

Henry Harris Jessup, Noeme Tabet

Letter forwarded by the American Missionaries of Beyrout, Lebanon, Tripoli, Sidon, etc.
To the Evangelical Native Church of Beyrout

ISBN/EAN: 9783337149055

Printed in Europe, USA, Canada, Australia, Japan

Cover: Foto ©ninafisch / pixelio.de

More available books at **www.hansebooks.com**

LETTER

FORWARDED BY THE AMERICAN

MISSIONARIES

OF

BEYROUT, LEBANON, TRIPOLI, SIDON, &c.

TO THE

EVANGELICAL NATIVE

CHURCH OF BEYROUT;

AND THE ANSWER

OF THE CHURCH TO IT.

———✦———

Beyrout, 28 February, 1898.

TRANSLATION OF THE
MISSIONARIES' LETTER.

To the

Committee and members of the Native Evangelical Church of Beyrout.

Dear brethren,

In presenting to you our brotherly salutations, we beg to say; — That a question was sent to us, through the perpetual secretary of our mission, demanding, whether we like to labour after uniting the two evangelical churches of Beyrout into one church, excluding the Presbyterian regulations: to which, we give the following answer.

We note with the greatest satisfaction the increase of affection between these two churches, and we do not overlook the great benefit which may accrue from their union; but we regret to find that it was made conditional on the seperation of one of them from being bound organically with her sister churches in the parishes of our mission, and from the organization of the neighbouring churches of other missions such as those of Egypt, Damascus, Shweir, and North Syria; and from the American churches which are carrying out missionary work in this land. And yet, all this, for the sake of union with a church which refrains form submitting to the Presbyterian code, without having actually tried it or refuted its validity by scriptural or rational proofs.

Consequently, on account of the existence of the Presbyterian code in the parishes which are under our control, it is no more left for us to judge in the questions relating to church administration, but to direct all such questions to the Presbyterian Conference, for deliberation, discussion, and decision.

Nevertheless, as our right is reserved to offer opinions and brotherly advice, we wish to remind the two churches of certain principles which we deem to be of vital importance in the forming and controlling of christian churches, and which also, we think, have been, somehow, neglected in both churches : —

1. It is necessary that each church should care for, and defray her own expenses as best as she can and as soon as she is able to do so. She is also requested to do her utmost to attain this end, even if it should cost her members, much self-denial, personally and collectively.

2. It is also necessary for each church, regarding her administration, to maintain the principle of judgment by majority of votes, very strictly and zealously ; for it is a fundamental principle for liberty and justice in the church.

3. Each church should hold in her own hands the control of her finances. She is urgently warned not to hand over this right to agents or committees, even if they were of her acting and legal members, unless they were properly elected by majority of votes, by which also, they

may be liable to be re-elected, changed or substituted by her own votes. When in office, they are responsible to her, next to God; and are bound to present and submit all their reports to her, to be examined and sanctioned.

4. Each church should unite with the other neighbouring churches who are sisters to her in faith; and should also be constitutionally bound to them, for by doing so, she would be well guarded and protected, and her outward service would be more improved and of greater influence.

Considering our respect for the liberty of the churches in managing their own affairs, we never think to be umpires in these churches; yet, we consider our relations with them so great, and important, and binding; and we deem their edification and progress, a matter of great interest and concern to us, that we are called upon to declare, that owing to long meditation, and careful communications, and wide experience, our confidence was greatly increased in the solidity of the Presbyterian code, which is now in practice in the evangelical churches of Syria, that it is the simplest in practice, the safest in guarding against dangers, and the most effectual in forwarding this interest and this growth.

Therefore, as one of the evangelical churches of Beyrout is now bound with the other churches by the presbyterian code, we need not repeat that it is no business of ours, to liberate her from this bond, neither is she able to do so herself, nor to carry out independently, any important project, without consulting the presbytery —: unless she wishes to encroach on the honour of her sister churches, to break her promises, her duties and pledges, and sever her relations which are brought to existence through the Presbyterian regulations.

It is considered that the greatest value and benefit of the Presbyterian Code, is, that it guards every church bound to it from plunging into hasty conclusions, which may be at variance with wisdom and justice.

Consequently, we rejoice that the Divine Providence has smoothed the path for the settlement of this question, very shortly, and in an agreeable way, through the meeting of the Presbyterian conference which will be held in Beyrout next April. For this conference is the legitimate representative of all rights and responsibilities which are for us, and against us in the control of decisions and church regulations.

This regency is affirmed, not only by the official reports of our mission, but also by the Acts of the old constitution, on which all the evangelical churches of this country were established.

Having expressed ourselves thus far, we conclude by invoking the blessing of the Head of the Church on you and your families, collectively; and may the grace, mercy and peace of the Father, the Son, and the Holy Ghost be with you all. Amen.

by order, and for the American mission,

Your brother,
H. H. JESSUP,
Gen. Sec.

To the Rev. Members of the American Mission in Beyrout, Lebanon, Tripoli and Sidon.

Dear and venerable brethren in the Risen Lord,

We beg to acknowledge the receipt of your letter dated the 20th. Dec. 1897, signed by your general and perpetual secretary in this country, and in which you express the hope to see the two Protestant Churches in Beyrout united into One. We, hereby, quote the following paragraph of your letter : —

« A question was sent to us, through the perpetual secretary of our mission, demanding, whether we like to labour after uniting the two evangelical churches of Beyrout, into one church, excluding the Presbyterian regulations: To which, we give the following answer.

« We note with the greatest satisfaction the increase of affection between these two churches, and we do not overlook the great benefit which may accrue form their union; but we regret to find that it was made conditional on the seperation of one of them from being bound organically with her sister churches in the parishes of our mission, and from the organization of the neighbouring churches of other mission; such as those of Egypt, Damascus, Shweir, and North Syria; and from the American churches which are carrying out missionary work in this land. And yet, all this, for the sake of union with a church which refrains from submitting to the Presbyterian code, without having actually tried it or refuted its validity by scriptural or rational proofs.

"Consequently, on account of the existence of the Presbyterian code in the parishes which are under our control, it is no more left for us to judge in the questions relating to church administration but to direct all such questions to the Presbyterian Conference, for deliberation, discussion, and decision."

These are the very words of your said letter and we beg to express our comments as follows: —

We were greatly astonished at the wording of this epistle that we hardly believed that it was written by your said secretary for two reasons: First, it was not signed by his own handwriting, and secondly, because it greatly differs from what he had announced to some members of our native church some time ago, when he asked them to attend a meeting expressly held for discussing the question of unity.

We, hereby, repeat his own words. "What prevents the two churches from uniting into one? If the Presbyterian code stands in the way, we can not see why it should not be put aside. What we aim at, is not the introduction and the carrying out of the said code, but that the church should maintain herself, and be independent." He also added, that he had communicated these views to all members of the mission including Rev. Dr. Eddy, and that all the answers were satisfactory, excepting two from Sidon field, who had not yet written. Even Rev. Mr. Marsh, of Tripoli, expressed his surprise that such a thing did not exist here as a Presbyterian code.

He has also expressed this fact; that the regulations of the said Presbyterian code of the church is not in practice, so that when two or three churches have actually become independent, they were free to act according to their own present circumstances and regulations. Then he added, that the secretary of the Presbyterian Board of America, who is an intelligent and prudent christian, and who has been on a visit to the East, has himself said, after strict investigation and experience, that the Presbyterian Code is quite unworkable in the churches of the Orient; and that the churches in Persia have preferred to follow the regulations of the Episcopal church; and that, were these churches forced to follow the

Presbyterian code, they would have been decayed and ruined.

He also added, that even the Board in America, to escape the enormous expenses which were incurred by the compulsory annual meetings, which amounted to 35,000 dollars, has decided to hold the general meeting once every three years, only.

Rev. Dr. H. Jessup, moreover, concluded by asking for the bill which was framed and signed by the members of the church, for the sake of peace, after years of discussion, to be presented and submitted to debate and discussion, as to whether it should be recognized and acted upon as a more preferable one.

We were very glad indeed to hear this venerable and beloved old secretary, Rev. Dr. Henry Jessup, express himself so openly and with so much competence upon the said subject, for he has always been wishing for the union of the two churches, as a father wishes to see his children with one accord united in peace and harmony.

On that declaration our hearts leaped with joy at the prospect of healing the sore wounds of our hearts, and we looked forward with the greatest longing to the time when the old unity should be resumed, and when we shall gather around the table of fellowship as one body, meeting in one church, and hearing the blessed news of the glorious Gospel preached from one pulpit.

Consequently, when we were expecting none less than these delightful news, your epistle came and foiled all our expectations, and destroyed, as it were, with one stroke, all hope for the desired unity, even our surprise was none less than our regret, and we found ourselves thus compelled to make manifest the following protests.

1. May we ask why did your Secretary declare for his own, and for you all, too, personally and collectively, such views as are above mentioned, when he was not sure of your unanimity ? Nevertheless, he affirmed that all your answers to his inquiry on the said question were favourable, excepting the two from the Sidon field whose answers had not yet come.

2. We quote from your letter to us, the following paragraph: « We have regretted to find that this union is dependent on the seperation of this church from the legal union with all sisterly churches in the parishes of your mission, also from the regulations of the neighbouring churches »

We must not conceal from you that the alleged union, though it be our heart's desire, was not proposed by us, nor did we ask to have it; (a) Because we have been enjoying the independence to which we were encouraged by yourselves, and you had long preached the necessity of it. (b) We were, thank God, enjoying both peace and edification in our independent church. (*c*) We were convinced, that it would be impossible for you to withdraw and to annul the same regulations which you were very anxious to introduce to the churches of your parishes. (*d*) we were confirmed in our belief which we learnt by years of experience, that nothing, however convincing, would dissuade you from carrying out your programme. You even refused any amendment for the moderation of your code of church - laws. Consequently, not being the seekers of the union we never made the seperation of our church from other churches a condition of our union, such as you have alluded to, in your letter.

In justifying the writing of your letter you said, that, A request was brought before you through your secretary, asking for the union of the two churches. May we ask who was the person who made that request?

3. The union of the two Evangelical Churches of Beyrout under the same old regulations established and sanctioned by your worthy predecessors the missionaries in this country, does not necessitate the abolition of your new organization, providing, that the other churches of Lebanon, Sidon and Tripoli, approve of it and acknowledge it as essential for their real interest. It does not also stand in the way of their annual meetings; but, on the contrary, they can exercise . their authority as they please, and who knows, whether we may be

influenced by them and follow their example, when we are convinced of the soundness of those assemblies by the increasing prosperity of those churches.

4. In saying that, we made a condition of our union the seperation of our church from being linked with her sister churches, you also added that this disunion means the seperation of our church from the American board which defrays the expenses of the mission, &c.

This reminds us of a speech delivered by one of you, in the Memorial Hall, not many years since, and which address has been printed in your printing press in Beyrout.

We quote here some passages of that famous address. « That the Presbyterian board pays liberally for our schools and printing presses, &c.; is it not a matter of propriety that we should obey its laws ? »

We confess, that we can not see the relation between an independent Church, or a church struggling for independence, whose members pay regularly all the fees for the education of their children, and the prices of books, &c., and who, like all christians, prefer to have the Gospel of Christ their only guide; and between the call of obedience to laws, of which they are totally ignorant, and which may not be of any benefit to them, to their church, and to their country. And what makes it more surpising is, to compare these ideas with what your late venerable secretary, Dr. Mitchell, said and affirmed before a large assembly, when he learned the gratifying tidings of our independence,which may be given in these words : « We do not attempt to bind you to the laws of a Presbyterian Board, nor to any other laws ; suffice it to say, that you have the Book of Life and the Spirit of God, together with the sound doctrines which you have imbibed from the old missionaries; what we now ask you is, to stick to those old doctrines and may the Lord richly bless your efforts.». We greatly rejoiced at that declaration.

We also add here what we have already quoted from the words of your secretary. He says, that experience and strict investigation have convinced him that the Presbyterian regulations will never do in the Orient.

If your own board, therefore, has liberated us from obeying these new laws, why should you now take the trouble to force upon us, the whole, unrevised, Presbyterian code ?

5. A paragraph in your letter reads thus : « And all that, was for the sake of a church which refuses to join her sisters which are bound to the Presbyterian organizations »

Why! this is extremely marvellous! Is it not worth while for a church, even a single, solitary one, to have the liberty and conscience of her members, recognised and respected ? Is it not of more consequence that it should preserve her peace and unity, and prefer these to all outer regulations of man ? Do you believe that such ordinances and laws are given by inspiration, or that they are absolutely necessary to salvation ? A good number of the dear old christians of our church have lived and died and never heard of your new laws ; can any one imagine that they have perished for not following your new organizations ? How far is this from the Apostle's words «Wherefore, if meat make my brother to offend, I will eat no flesh while the world standeth, lest I make my brother to offend,» and also, « And unto the Jews I become as a Jew, that I might gain the Jews, &c. » and also «Who is weak and I am not weak? who is offended, and I burn not, &c. ? » and also, « Stand ye therefore in the liberty wherewith Christ hath made us free, and be not entangled again with the yoke of bondage.» If we therefore, look to the word of God as the only light which we are exhorted to follow, we find that edification, union, fellowship, harmony in faith and good works among members of the church, are far more necessary and of more vital importance than all the laws of men put together.

6. You exhort the two churches of Beyrout to unite and become independent, and at the same time you insist upon introducing your whole code of laws. If, therefore, we have carried on our own independence and have spared you the

pains of tutelage and expenses; have we not the right to abide by the old rules in which most of us were born and bred from childhood, ? Are we not entitled to remain faithful to them? Are you not aware that your same new code differs in certain churches from others ? There is some difference between the churches of Damascus, Lattakia, & Egypt and that of your Board in America. Also the churches of Scotland have not quite the same views as those of France and America. Even your venerable secretary, said, « that the Presbyterian code which has been founded in Syria, is but a dim shadow of the practical reality, and that when two or three churches agree together they can work out their own laws.

Why is it that you exhort us to be independent, while at the same time you lay obstacles in the way of our independence, and wish us to submit to regulations the most important of which are still quite unknown to us ?

7. You say. « Our church did not actually try the Presbyterian ordinances, neither did it refute its validity by scriptural or moral proofs. » May we ask, did you refute the soundness of our old constitution, which was organized by your predecessors, by the same evidences ? Did you point out the dangers of its use by undoubted facts ? or, have you established your new organization by such convincing arguments which leave no place for doubt ? Or, Have you submitted this new

code to our perusal and study in order to be convinced, or at least reconciled to it ? For, how could we accept or refuse a thing which is kept in your book-cases in big volumes ? It was only proper that you should translate these books into our native tongue, or at least, the principal part of them, in order that we may study their contents closely, and either sanction or refute their validity. Then you would have the right to organize those that accept it into one constitutional party, and leave the others to exercise their faith in their old conservative way, according to the dictates of their hearts and conscience. You would, therefore, have thus done the proper and the right thing, leaving no ground for suspicion, discord, and dismemberment.

We fail not to declare, that we have searched the Scriptures all through, and we never came across any commandment binding on christians to hold up annual meetings of parishes, and conferences of synods, and universal meetings; neither did we hit upon any reference to them, excepting the meeting of the apostles and elders in Jerusalem to decide upon a scriptural controversy which had, at that time, disturbed the peace of the church of Antioch, and which caused disagreement among believers of both Jews and Gentiles regarding cirumcision. We learn that the church sent Paul and Barnabas to Jerusalem to ask for the opinion of the Apostles and elders.

They gave out their judgment, by the inspiration of the Holy Ghost, that the believers should be excused from this ordinance which Christ has abolished with all other old Testament ones. We understand by this, that the apostles, and only they, have the right to decide in such matters, owing to the inspiration, and the particular authority which were given them. We did not find that representatives of the churches of Cæsarea, Jaffa, Lydda and Damascus, were also present. And besides, this is the only conference that was thus held as is understood from the book of the Acts of the Apostles. No mention, whatever, is made of any meeting of the envoys of the churches of Palestine, Asia Minor, Greece, Macedonia, and others. Neither did Christ order the annual meetings of the Apostles for making new binding rules which may serve to entangle and to burden the churches and make them groan under a heavy and quite unnecessary yoke.

We could not make out what solid basis you propose to put for this new organization, unless you had for an example the Jewish synagogue of the seventy (which assembly sentenced our Saviour to the death of the cross), to which you refer in an article published in the "Neshra", your religious weekly paper, about two years since. We have much to say about this for comment, but we would rather postpone our observations until we are somewhat acquainted with the details of these regulations.

8. During the long years of controversy which arose between us on account of this subject, we asked you to point out the reasons which called you to introduce the said code. You gave those reasons and we noted them down on paper. After slight alterations, we accepted the bill for sheer love of peace, and for the sake of keeping unity and harmony in the church. The members of the church also applied their signatures to this bill and accepted it by vote, unanimously. Then your secretary signed it too.

Its acceptance by both sides put a stop for a time to our long discussions. After all that, you dropped the bill as if it never existed, and came forward to force the whole of the Presbyterian code upon us. If the first bill which we accepted after revision was alone the Presbyterian code, why have you neglected it, and laid it aside? and if it was not, why did you not say so at the time? Your secretary gave out in the sitting which was held at his request for discussing the question of union — « that the afore-mentioned bill does not differ from the whole code except in one rule, *viz.*, that the code demands that the meetings should be held annually while the bill leaves it open for the time of need.

May we ask now ; if there was no serious reason that the

churches should meet, why the trouble of summoning the delegates and incur the pains and expenses of travel, and the loss of precious time, &c. ? Should those deputations incur such unnecessary trouble and expenses for no important reasons, will not their meetings thus be the means for new disappointments and controversies which we must try to avoid ?

Will not this also lead to disscusions which will bring forth satires and place the church in a critical position which she had no business to have come to ? Do not our old rules give us the right to summon deputations of churches in time of need, for the settling of all prominent questions ? Why should we, therefore, who are weak and few in number, entangle ourselves with such burdens and incur such expenses, which even the rich churches of America could not bear ? for such was the information given us by your secretary who is striving after this union.

9. You say that, "On account of the presence of the Presbyterian code in the parishes which are under your control you can not give your judgment in any question. connected with the control of their affairs, but that you have to lay all such questions before the Presbyterian conference to discuss and settle."

We believe that this matter is entirely confined to

your own hands, because those churches know nothing of these ordinances which you have pressed upon them, and which may only entangle and crush their liberty. We confess, that we are almost ignorant of them, and we are assured that most, if not all the members of those churches, know no more about them than the fixing of the time of their meeting in a particular place. Even if they were asked as to what they were going to do in these meetings, they would say, that they do not know. For, what can they say of a code which is scarely known? We might also go far as to say, that a good number of its supporters know next to nothing of its various articles. We were surprised to read in your letter that those parishes were under your control, and yet you can not give any decisive opinion in the questions that are laid before you. Have you not the majority of votes? or, is it not you who pronounce the decision? What is more worth noticing is, that you are its most influential members, and are also the judges of others who offend or violate the law; but as to the members of your mission, they are exempted from the power of these laws. This stands in contradiction to all laws of churches and tribunals, for it widely differs from justice. In short, you are able to unite the two churches in one day, had you only the will to do it.

Thank God, there are no enmities, nor hatred, nor spites,

nor grudges, between members of both churches, and there is no reason that justifies this seperation. We love our brethren of the other church and honour them, and many of both congregations pray for this greatly desired union, for most of them have been brought up in the old constitution since their infancy. Why do you drive us away from our inheritance and portion in Israel, and deprive us from the privilege of enjoying our dear brotherly fellowship? We are, as you know, a small and weak congregation, that has suffered much, and borne reproach for the love of Christ our Saviour and His Gospel of Truth. Is it not enough that we should be alienated from our people and friends? Is it not enough that we have borne the severe judgment of those from without? Is it not sufficient that we are deprived of our representative rights before the government? Are you not the preachers of the Gospel of peace, and the heralds of the God of Love, and servants of Him who gave His Life to unite in one body all that are saved, of both Jews and Gentiles? If we do not look to you for restoration of peace and reconciliation according to the will of Him who reconciled us by the blood of His cross, who will do it?

10. You said in the first Article of your exhortation "That it is necessary that each church should provide for its own self as best she could, and that she is urgently

asked to do her uttermost to attain this object, even if its members have to deny themselves, personally and collectively." What we now answer to this is; that by the Grace of God we have achieved this end, and have spared you the pains of admonition. Yes, thank God, we have become the first fruits of the churches of Syria in this respect. And we fervently pray, that all those churches should seek after this end and be enabled to follow our example. Their independence will be a source of joy to our hearts. Notwithstanding, we do thank you for your kind advice, and pray that our Father will give us strength according to our need.

11. In your epistle this paragraph is also included, — « It is very necessary for every church to hold up, very zealously and minutely, the principle of deciding all questions by majority of votes, in all matters which affect her administration. » For this principle, « is a fundamental part of Liberty and Justice in the Church. »

It is true that this is a proved fact in all constitutional affairs. We have stood by it, and for it, and we mean to abide by this rule. But to yield to the votes of members of the church, who are strangers and whose stay in our midst is temporal, and who know very little of the particular affairs of the church ; And also the yielding to votes of members who do not participate nor subscribe to defray expenses of the church, etc., is a question that deserves the utmost consideration, in order to have it settled in such a proper way, that will not affect the interest and prosperity of the Church.

We were more surprised when you said that, « It is necessary for every church to hold up the principle of decision by majority of votes ; And that, after strict investigation, you were convinced that the Presbyterian code is most simple in practice, etc." May we ask with which church did you enter into communication in this respect ? or, whether you have gained the majority of votes of the Beyrout Church, whose members are above a hundred ? Did you ask for the votes of the other churches, and have you legally obtained the majority ? What strange problem ! How do you exhort us to stick to a law which you yourselves violate ? If you have only gained the majority of your own missionary votes, not heeding the churches, will that be called a law of justice ?

12. Your third Article reads thus : "It is indispensable that each church should manage her own finance, which, should never be entrusted to a committee or to representatives, even if they were church active members, unless they are properly elected by majority of votes, and that those elected by majority are liable to be changed. They are also pledged to present to the church

all their reports to be sanctioned; and they are, to *her*, next to God, responsible in all things.»

What we have to say now is, that this is exactly what we are doing, and what we intend to adhere to, except the control of bequeathed cash and property when left by the testator under the charge of the Church's Benevolent Society. If the testator wills that his bequest should be entrusted to such Society, then this body is obliged to carry out the charge. We cannot see how can the society take the liberty to violate the will, and hand over what she was entrusted with, to the church, thus opposing the will of the testator.

13. In your fourth Article we read that, « It is incumbent on every church to be united to the neighbouring sister churches, and to be linked with them in a most binding manner; first, to guarantee her own security; and secondly, to be able to raise and improve herself, and to have more influence in her service with those who are without.»

Our answer is this: We have been united to our sister churches for a period of about 50 years, acknowledging *one* simple constitution laid down by the first venerable missionaries. No dissension, whatever, arose between us; and the bond of christian love and harmony linked us all together. We had no trouble that led to dismemberment, neither had we any perversion of our creed which we have embraced and pledged ourselves solemnly to keep and protect since our admission into the fellowship of the Church. All that we wish for is, to have those solemn vows respected and not endangered by adding any supplements. Let it not be supposed that we are opposed to all organizations, but let it be understood that we deem it of vital importance to abide by the constitution which we have accepted and promised to hold; for that is the only security for the maintenance of the church, and the link that binds our unity, also the best means for the improvement and increase of the Church's influence in her service amongst those without. We never wished to be separated from our sister churches, and we think that separation is a most deplorable misfortune to the church, and ought to be avoided by all possible means. We welcome all members of Christian churches who desire to see us; and we most heartily wish to have concord and harmony and brotherly discussion of all questions for the good of the church and her prosperity.

14. We also quote this: that « While standing for the liberty of all churches to manage their own affairs, you never dreamt of occupying in them the post of umpires; but, having much and important relations with them, and watching over their progress with a loving heart, you deem it incumbent upon you to make this declaration that, after much reflection

and correspondence, and sound experience, you have come to this firm conclusiont, hat the Presbyterian code, which is in use at present in the churches of Syria, is the simplest in practice, the safest in averting dangers, and the most effectual for the good and progress of the churches. »

Here, we if would we could hold our peace, for we are not in an attitude of sharp controversy, neither can we comment on a code the greater part of which is not known, but is contained in huge volumes which have made even your Board fail to make of it an abbreviated summary. If you say that this code has been translated into our language and printed, we would affirm that this little tract is but a shadow of the original, proving this from the words of a member of your mission.

What is already translated is of little or no consequence. It is astonishing to hear you saying, « It is of the simplest of constitutions », when it is ascertained that it contains many parts and chapters which can only be learnt after a long time of laborious study. We consequently, have pleasure in informing you that the constitution which we have known, accepted, and held since the birth of the church in Syria, is simpler still, and we found no defects nor faults in it, and so, we shall hold on to it as long as we are sure of its solidity. You say that the Presbyterian code is safer and more effectual, etc.; but you have not given us any valid proofs. Neither did we note any progress of the churches who embraced it, nor their growth in spiritual matters. On the contrary, we have noted with sorrow the dissensions that sprang up in the churches after its introduction, such as have happened in Miniara (Tripoli field), Zahleh, Hasbeya, Judeida, and Sidon. Even the conference which was held last year in Sidon has not been represented by three churches, who are the most important in that field, and it has passed its vote even in the absence of a good number of the representatives of the sister churches. We can not tell how far this discord would reach in the future, but is this not a sufficient proof that we ought not to accept codes that breed dissensions ? You did not point out to us the weakness and the supposed dangers of our constitution, but facts prove that it is more safe and solid.

You will kindly allow us, in speaking of the « Presbyterian code », to say, that the word Presbytery which you attribute to this code is taken from St. Paul's Epistle to Timothy 1 Tim. IV : 14. « Neglect not the gift that is in thee, which was given thee by prophecy, with the laying on of the hands of the Presbytery. » But this word stands for ministers or elders or those advanced in years and experience in Spiritual Knowledge. These men, never laid a written code of regulations for the churches, neither did they ordain binding annual meetings for parishes, nor universal conferences. Moreover, we were greatly surprised by your adding a fourth order to the church service, *viz.*, ruling elders whom you place on a level with ministers, and ordain them to permanent office. You are aware that the Apostle in writing to the Philippians said, « To all the saints with the Bishops (or ministers or elders as explained in the marginal notes of the Bible), and deacons. »

Had there been a fourth grade, the Apostle would have never hesitated to mention it. But if you quote the text « Let the elders that rule well, be counted worthy of double honour, » we answer that the word rule is an attribute of the elders or pastors who are foremost in their experience, owing to their advance in age, and not a special grade or office in the church. It is well known that some of the church members, have the gifts of administration or rule, as others have the gifts of instruction, of interpretation, etc. We can not therefore admit that whoever obtains these gifts should necessarily be counted as one of the permanent office bearers, unless you deem it only a matter of convenience. Consequently, if we have only our own convenience to think of, not heeding the Book of Life, we open the door for superfluous dogmas, which may have an undesirable end. Moreover, if the elders be of the same grade as ministers, never to be changed or removed as is the case in the Presbyterian code, the result would be that all the members of these conferences would stand as one ministerial grade and the people would be left unrepresented. The conference being shut to every one except ministers and elders, and consequently the church will be deprived of the liberty of electing its representatives.

You said that you never intended to be umpires in churches; if so, why not leave to our two Evangelical churches in Beyrout the liberty of union? Or, why do you not exhort and help us to realize it, as is expected from preachers who consider the higher interest of the church as the most important and binding duty, as you have expressed it in your letter. We know that you are very influential in those churches, and we never imagine that they will oppose you, if you really desire to have the union, but, on the contrary, all will help you to accomplish it.

15. You said also, « That as one of the two Evangelical churches in Beyrout is now united with the other churches in the Presbyterian form, it is a matter of fact that freeing her of this bond is beyond your power ; even this said church, can never break this link, nor carry out any important undertaking before consulting the Presbyterian conference. If she did anything without consultation, she would violate her pledges and duties towards her sister churches. You say also that the

chief benefit of the Presbyterian code, is to guard every church which adopts it from falling into needless changes, which may be both unwise and unjust.» In answer to which, we say; that the mutual union between the members of one church is more essential than their connexion with other churches. And yet those which you name as « the two Evangelical churches of Beyrout » are in reality only one church, and it grieves our hearts to hear them called two. It is true that one part of this church has stood aloof for some particular reasons, which certainly have not been caused by the members themselves, but we never despaired of a speedy reconciliation; for the members of both parties were united for not less than fifty years, and we are sure that their christian, brotherly, and natural union is far more binding than the connexion of one part with the Presbyterian convention for the short period of two years only. Nevertheless, this said connexion does not include all the members, the majority of whom have scarcely known any thing of this assembly, its condition, and consequences; and in which the church was only represented by one minister and one elder, and no more. It would have been far better to unite first the two parties, enabling them to carry out the independence for which you have so often exhorted us, and which both you and your board deem a primary and vital measure, than to bring forward your new code with its various and full explanations, leaving to us the liberty of accepting, modifying, or refusing it. Especially, as your American Board gives its advice to this effect, as we were made to understand this from your two worthy secretaries the late Rev. Dr. Mitchell, and the present secretary, both men of wisdom, intelligence and experience.

In regard to your saying, « It does not concern you to free our sister church from this connexion, » we have already given you our answer. We did not ask you to liberate, but we request you to grant us the liberty of choice and action. We have reasons to believe that if not all the brethren of the other church, the majority at least would rather have this union had their free will been respected. For there are no personal causes which justify this separation, neither did they see in their former code anything which would lead them to abandon it and embrace the Presbyterian regulation. In speaking of our sister church you say, « that you can not sever this link, nor can she, independently, carry out any important undertaking unless she consults the presbyterian assembly. If she does anything without consultation she would infringe the law of respect to her sister churches, and break her promises and pledges with the presbyterian confederation.» This was greatly surprising to us; can not a church carry out an important project without being forced to consult other churches who may not approve of it ? Where is then the liberty to which Christ hath called us ? It seems, that you have chained the hands of the churches, and prevented them from carrying on their own progress and endeavouring to act for their benefit and interest. Supposing the presbyterian conference was held in April, and in May the church thought of an important undertaking which she may deem most necessary for her benefit; must she then postpone the matter eleven months and wait for the second meeting of the convention in order to lay her proposals before that body, perhaps to find that it was too late ? If that be the case, we must confess that this code instead of being an attraction to us is rather a repulsion. It drives us away in order that we may not bind ourselves with chains which we can not bear. We even doubt whether our brethren in the other church knew of these regulations and whether they submitted to them; any how, we know, that they, as well as we, have the full liberty to choose what we find most conducive to the welfare of our church. And we doubt not, that while you are the representatives and defenders of religious freedom, you will never encourage us to part with such liberty.

16. The end of your letter has the following, « We are glad that the Divine Providence has smoothed the way for an agreeable and speedy solution of this question through the

Presbyterian assembly, which is to hold its sitting in Beyrout, next April. For this conference is the legitimate representative of all rights and responsibilities, for and against you in the Church's administration and constitution, as this regency is corroborated not only by the official programmes of your Mission, but also by the old constitution on the basis of which all the churches of this country are built ».

We believe that the Divine Providence facilitates, at all times, peace and union, when there is sincerity and honesty, and when all stumbling blocks are cast aside. And we do not imagine that our brethren, the members of the conference, desire the separation of our church, for we still know them to be full of Christian love and Christian zeal, and this gives us strong hope of their good will towards us.

You say, « That this regency is corroborated not only by the official programmes of your mission but also by the old constitution on the basis of which all the Evangelical churches of this country were established. »

We were very glad to hear you say so ; and we are ready to submit to this paragraph, « That the Evengelical Churches of this country were established on the old constitution. » Well, the said constitution says, « That if any difficulty occurs in a church, the Committee of which is unable to solve, she has the right to call Pastors and representatives of the sister churches to help her in the solution of that difficulty.» We do not believe that our church has yet failed to solve the present question, for she did not yet meet officially to discuss and decide it. But, should she meet once or twice for deep study and exchange of opinions and fail, then she would seek the assistance of brother pastors and representatives of the other churches.

You say our church is established on this solid constitution, therefore she will remain faithful to it and abide by it in accordance with the conviction of her conscience, and to avoid the criticism of other denominations.

In submitting these remarks to you, we beg to say, that we have not been actuated by any mere selfish motives nor by any prejudices. God forbid ! We never thought of undervaluing the honour and respect due to you, but, on the contrary, we greatly appreciate your missionary, benevolent, and literary efforts, for which we cannot but express our sincere thanks both to you and to your board in America.

We believe that our present difference does not affect our common belief in the solemn principles of our Lord's living Word, nor our aims towards edification, growth in spiritual life, and spreading the word of our common Master in our beloved country. For, how can we disagree about apparel and leave the living body to suffer and emaciate. If my partner should disagree with me on a question of apparel or fashion of dress, I do not see why I should quarrel with him and sever my friendly connexion for such a trifling cause.

We believe that should the union of these two parts of the one church in one place of worship be unfortunately unattainable, the union of their hearts in a Christian bond of love and the keeping up of brotherly relationship will not be, by God's blessing, impossible. We see Evangelical Churches in America, England, etc., doing their utmost for establishing closer relationship between christians, and it is mostly for this end that they form committees and hold conferences and conventions for deepening the christian life, and for stronger fellowship in forwarding Christ's Kingdom. Why should we not follow their example ? Do we not believe in one Saviour, and partake of the same evangelical truths ? Have we not one end in view, one hope, and look for one home in heaven ? Let no one, therefore, say I am of Paul's or Apollos', or Cephas', for we are all the body of Christ, and members in particular. We had no other motives in framing these comments, than to disclose to you our hearts as to venerable and zealous pastors who aim after the harmony, the peace, and the independence of the church, and who have also greatly laboured, in planting the seed of the saving truth in this country. We rejoice to see this seed taking root, and growing. You have infused into these infant Protestant churches in Syria, those precious gospel principles which helped her to grow and by which we desire to abide. We do not at all think that you desire any dismemberment of the church; consequently, we hope that you will help us to heal these wounds, and unite in peace and harmony in one place of worship.

Before coming to a close, we call upon the Head of our Church, to guide us, one and all, into the path of reconciliation and charity, to point out to us the more effective means for the overcoming of all obstacles that block the way of progress in His Kingdom and the prosperity of His Church.

We also call upon our brethren and sisters of our church in Beyrout, (not saying, "the other church"), and also all the Evangelical churches of Syria, that they may unite together, in assisting us with their prayers and advice, that we may attain this most desirable object, *viz.,* Perfect union and harmony, under the All-Surrounding wings and the All-Powerful Arms of Our Lord and master, Jesus Christ, and the influence of His Holy Spirit; for which we all, unanimously and fervently pray. Amen.

By order of the Evangelical Native
Church of Beyrout and its Committee,
Nœmé Tabet,
Deacon.

www.ingramcontent.com/pod-product-compliance
Lightning Source LLC
Chambersburg PA
CBHW030719110426
42739CB00030B/978

صورة

اللائحة المُرسَلَة من حضرات المُرسَلين الامركيين الافاضل

فـِي

بيروت ولبنان وحقلَي طرابلس وصيدا

الى

الكنيسة الانجيلية الوطنية الثابتة على نظامها الاستقلالي المؤسسة عليهِ منذ نحو ٦٠ سنة في شأن انضمامها الى الكنيسة الامركية التي تبعت حديثًا النظام المشيخي وجواب الكنيسة الوطنية عليها

‏------‏

﷽ اللائحة ﷽

جناب الأفاضل الأعزاء عمدة وأعضاء كنيسة بيروت الإنجيلية الوطنية المحترمين

غب اهدائكم التحيات الأخوية نبدي انه قد ورد لنا سؤال عن يد كاتب ارساليتنا الدائم ان كنا نريد ان نسعى في انضمام الكنيستين الانجيليتين في بيروت الى كنيسة واحدة خارجة عن النظام المشيخي فعليه نجيب . بان نرى بملء السرور كل ازدياد في الالفة فيما بين هاتين الكنيستين ولسنا متغافلين عن الفوائد العظيمة التي يؤمل الحصول عليها بواسطة انضمامهما الواحدة للاخرى . غير اننا نرى باسف انه مشروط في هذا الانضمام فصل الواحدة منهما عن الارتباط النظامي مع اخواتها الكنائس اجمالا اي في ابرشيات ارساليتنا . كما وعن نظام الكنائس المجاورة لنا والمتعلقة بارساليات اخرى كالتي في مصر والشام والشوير وجهات سوريا الشمالية . وايضا عن الكنائس الاميركية القائمة بمهام التبشير في هذه البلاد . وكل ذلك لاجل الانضمام الى كنيسة واحدة التي تأبى الارتباط بالنظام المشيخي بدون ان تكون قد امتحنته فعليا او افسدت صحنه ببراهين انجيلية او عقلية فبناء على وجود النظام المشيخي في الابرشيات التي هي تحت ادارتنا ليس لنا بعد ان نحكم بالمسائل المتعلقة بالنظام الكنسي بل يتوجب علينا احالة كل هذه المسائل الى المجمع المشيخي لاجل التبصر والحكم فيها

٣

ولكن لكون حقنا محفوظ في تقديم الاراء والنصائح الاخوية٠٠ نزيد
ان نذكّر الكنيستين ببعض المبادىء التي نعدّها ضرورية للغاية في تأليف
وادارة الكنائس المسيحية والتي نحسب انها نالت بعض الاهمال في هاتين
الكنيستين

اولاً انه يتوجب على كل كنيسة ان تقوم بكامل مصروفها بنفسها
بقدر ما يمكنها وباول ما يمكنها ذلك وان تبذل قصارى الجهد في الوصول
الى هذا المقصود ولو افضى الامر الى انكار الذات الكلي من اعضائها
افرادًا واجمالاً

ثانيًا انه يتوجب على كل كنيسة ان تحافظ بكل غيرة ودقة على
مبدإ الاعتماد على الحكم باكثرية الاصوات في ادارة شوؤونها لكون هذا
المبدإ هو من اركان الحرّية والانصاف في الكنيسة

ثالثًا انه يتوجب على كل كنيسة ان تحفظ بيدها ادارة ماليتها ولا
يسوغ لها مطلقًا تسليم هذه الادارة ليد وكلاء او لجنة او جمعية ولو من
اعضائها القانونيين ان لم يكونوا هولاء قد أُقيموا لذلك بانتخابها الحرّ وقابلين
للتجديد والتنزيل والتبديل باصواتها وهي ومكلّفين بتقديم كل تقريراتهم لها
لاجل المصادقة ومسوؤلين لها في كل شيء بعد٠ مسوؤليتهم لله

رابعًا انه يتوجب على كل كنيسة الانضمام الى سائر الكنائس المخاوية
لها بالايمان والمجاورة لها والارتباط النظامي الاشدّ ما يمكن معها اولاً لاجل
صيانتها ثم لاجل زيادة التحسين والتأثير في خدمتها الخارجية

وبالاجمال نقول انه مع محافظتنا على حرية الكنائس في ادارة
شوؤونها بحيث لا يخطر لنا على بال ان نحكم فيها فاننا نحسب علاقاتنا معها
كثيرة ومهمة وشديدة ونعتبر صالحها ونموها من اعزّ واعظم الامور عندنا
ولذلك نصرّح لها انه بعد تأملات كثيرة ومخابرات مستوفية واخبارات
متسعة قد زاد يقيننا بان النظام المشيخي الجاري الان في الكنائس السورية

الانجيلية اجمالاً هو ابسط ما يكون في المارسة واسلم ما يكون من الاخطار وافضل ما يكون في خدمة هذا الصالح وهذا النمو

و بما ان احدى الكنيستين الانجيليتين في بيروت هي الان متحدة مع الكنائس الاخرى في النظام المشيخي فالامر غني عن البيان بانهُ ليس بعد من خصائصنا حلّها من هذا الارتباط كما وانها هي لا نقدر ان تفسخ هذه العلاقة ولا ان تقوم بمشروع مهم مستقلة بدون استشارة المجمع المشيخي الا وتكون قد مسّت ناموس الكنائس اخواتها وواجباتها وعهودها الناجمة عن علاقاتها المشيخية · وانهُ يُعدّ من اعظم فوائد النظام المشيخي ان يُعين على وقاية كل كنيسة مرتبطة بهذا النظام من الوقوع في تغييرات عجولة او مغايرة للحكمة او العدالة

فالان نسرّ بان العناية الالهية قد سهلت السبيل لحل هذه المسألة في وقت غير بعيد وبطريقة جميلة بواسطة الاجتماع المشيخي المعين انعقادهُ في بيروت في نيسان القادم · لان هذا المجمع هو الوارث القانوني لكافة الحقوق والمسؤولية التي كانت لنا وعلينا في ادارة الاحكام والنظامات الكنائسية وهذه الخلافة مؤبدة ليس فقط بتقريرات ارساليتنا الرسمية بل ايضًا بموجب بنود النظام القديم الذي تأسست عليه الكنائس الانجيلية في هذه البلاد

هذا ما لزم تقديمهُ مع طلب بركة راس الكنيسة الوحيد عليكم وعلى عيالكم جميعًا — ونعمة ورحمة وسلام من الاب والابن والروح القدس مع جميعكم · امين

بيروت في ٢٠ ك١ سنة ٩٧

بامر المرسلين الامركيين
وبالنيابة عنهم
اخوكم
هنري جسب
الكاتب العام

﴿ الجواب ﴾

حضرات الافاضل الموقرين اعضاء الارسالية الامريكية في بيروت ولبنان وطرابلس وصيدا المحترمين

بملء السرور نرفع لمقامكم العالي اعتباراتنا القلبية مقرونة باحتراماتنا الفائقة لحضرتكم • وبعده فقد ظفرنا برقيمكم الكريم المتضمن " ورود سؤال لحضراتكم عن يد جناب كاتب ارساليتكم الدائم مفاده ُ — ان كنتم تريدون السعي في انضمام الكنيستين الانجيليتين في بيروت الى كنيسة واحدة خارجة عن النظام المشيخي وانكم تجيبون بابداء سرورکم من هذا الانضام وانكم لستم متغافلين عن الفوائد العظيمة التي يؤمل الحصول عليها بواسطة هذا الانضمام " ثم اردفتم ذلك بقولكم " انكم رأيتم باسف انه ُ مشروط في هذا الانضمام فصل الواحدة منهما عن الارتباط النظامي مع اخواتها الكنائس اجمالاً في ابرشيات ارساليتكم كما وعن نظام الكنائس المجاورة والمتعلقة بارساليات اخرى كالتي في مصر والشام والشوير وجهات سوريا الشمالية كما وعن الكنائس الامريكية القائمة بمهام التبشير في هذه البلاد وكل ذلك لاجل الانضمام الى كنيسة واحدة التي تأبى الارتباط بالنظام المشيخي بدون ان تكون قد امتحنته ُ فعلياً او افسدت صحنه ُ ببراهين انجيلية او عقلية • فبناء على وجود النظام المشيخي في الابرشيات التي هي تحت ادارتكم ليس

لكم بعد ان تحكموا بالمسائل المتعلقة بالنظام الكنسي بل يتوجب عليكم
احالة كل هذه المسائل الى المجمع المشيخي لاجل التبصّر والحكم فيها »
وعلى ذلك نجيب ، انّا لقد دُهشنا من نص رسالتكم هذه ولم نكد
نصدق انها من حضرة كاتب ارساليتكم الموقَّر لكونها غير موقعة بخط يده
ولانها جاءت كل المعاكسة لما حادث به بعض اعضاء كنيستنا
عندما دعاهم للمذاكرة بمسألة الانضمام التي تهمّنا كثيرًا كما انها تهمّنا ايضًا
فممّا قاله حينئذٍ « ما المانع من انضمام الكنيستين ؟ فاذا كان النظام المشيخي
يمنع من تحقيق هذه الغاية لا نرى سببًا يحول دون القائه ، وان الغاية
الاولى عندنا ليست في مسألة النظام بل استقلال الكنيسة وقيامها بنفقاتها
الخاصّة. وانه فاوض اعضاء الارسالية بذلك ومنهم جناب الدكتور ادي
فورد له منهم جواب الاستحسان خلا اثنين من حقل صيدا . وان جناب
المستر مارش من حقل طرابلس كتب له مظهرًا عجبهُ من الالماع الى
النظام المشيخي بمعنى ان النظام المذكور ليس جاريًا الان في الكنائس ،
وان النظام الحالي لا يحق ان يُدعى نظامًا مشيخيًا . ، وممّا قاله ايضًا « ان
ما اخذنا بالسير عليه الان يُدعى رسمًا لا حقيقة وانه متى استقلّت كنيستان
او ثلاث تسنّ لنفسها النظام الذي تختاره » ثم اردف ذلك بقوله « ان
حضرة كاتم اسرار المجمع في امركا وهو شاب ذكي حكيم ساح في الشرق
مدة فرأى بعد الاختبار وامعان النظر ان نظام امركا المشيخي لا ينطبق على
مصلحة الكنائس في الشرق حتى ان الكنائس في بلاد العجم طلبت ان تسير
على النظام الاسقفي ولو سارت على المشيخي لعراها الهبوط والانحطاط.
وقال ايضًا ان المجمع في امركا نفسها لما رأى كثرة النفقات التي تكبّدها
البالغة ٣٥ الف ريال استصوب عقد المجمع في كل ثلاث سنين بدلًا من
كل سنة « ثم ختم كلامه بالسؤال عن اللائحة التي وقّعتها الكنيسة باجماع
الاراء واحد اعضاء الميشن منذ بضع سنين بعد البحث والمذاكرة بهذا

الموضوع اعوامًا ليُنظرَ فيها اذا كان يمكن الجري عليها • والخلاصة ان حضرتهُ شديد الرغبة في انضمام الكنيستين لاسباب كثيرة اهمها حبهُ الشديد لكل فرد من الكنيستين وحبهم لهُ اذ يحسبونهُ كوالد وهو يحسبهم كاولاده • فسررنا جدًا من نبإ هذا القس الفاضل الدكتور هنري جسب وشكرنا لهُ حُسن نيتهِ وغبرتهِ كل الشكر وطارت قلوبنا فرحًا بوشك اندمال الجراح واستئناف الاشتراك الاخوي في كنيسة واحدة ومنبر واحد ومائدة واحدة الامر الذي ظمئت قلوبنا لتحقيقه كل الظماء • وبينا نحن نتوقع بشوق لا مزيد عليه الفوز بهذا الارب واذا برسالتكم وردت علينا فحيّرتنا واحبطت آمالنا ولم نَرْبَدّ من ابداء احتجاجنا واسفنا لحضراتكم والاجابة عنها بما خطر لنا راجين ان تفسحوا لنا مجالاً للعذر والترويِّ فيها نعرضهُ

اولاً • قد استغربنا كل الاستغراب مفاتحة حضرة كاتب ارساليتكم اِيانا بالمسألة وهو على غير يقين من استحسان سائر اعضاء ارساليتكم ومصادقتهم • على انهُ انبأنا عن استعلامهِ من اكثركم وورود اجوبة ملائمة لسؤاله

ثانيًا • عجبنا ايضًا من قولكم « انكم رأيتم باسف انهُ مشروط في هذا الانضمام فصل الكنيسة الواحدة عن الارتباط النظامي مع اخواتها الكنائس اجمالاً في ابرشيات ارساليتكم كما وعن نظام الكنائس المجاورة الخ » لان هذا الانضمام وان كان مما يسرّنا جدًا و يؤدي الى زيادة البنيان والتآزُر الاخوي لم نطلبهُ ولم نسعَ لاجله لفوزنا بالاستقلال الذي طالما نوّهتم بهِ وكرمتم علينا الحث لاجلهِ • ولكوننا شكرًا لله ظافرين بالراحة والفائدة الروحية في كنيستنا المستقلّة • ولعلنا بتعذُّر عدولكم عن تتميم المجمع في سائر الابرشيات التي تحت ادارتكم • ولانتقاد علمنا بالاختبار بمداعوام قضيناها بالابحاث والمناقشات بهذا الموضوع اقلهُ لاجل تعديل انظمة المجمع المذكور

انكم لا تحولون عن عزمكم قط · ولما كان الطالبين لم نكن نشترط قط فصل الكنيسة عن ذلك الارتباط الذي اشرتم اليه · وقد ذكرتم انه ورد لكم سؤال عن يد كاتب ارسالتكم بطلب الانضمام فممّن ياتُرى كان هذا السؤال ؟

ثالثًا · ان انضمام كنيسي بيروت الانجيليتين تحت نظامهما السابق المسنون من حضرات المشن الافاضل سلفائكم لا يستلزم الغاء انعقاد مجامعكم في الابرشيات الاخرى كلبنان وصيدا وطرابلس اذا شاءت تلك الكنائس قبول النظام الحديث · بل ربما كان التئامها حاملاً ابانا على الاقتداء بها في الاستقبال متى اطلعنا تمام الاطلاع على تلك الانظمة وشاهدنا فعلاً نجاح تلك الكنائس تحت النظام المذكور

رابعًا · في معرض ذكركم أنا اشترطنا في هذا الانضمام فصل الكنيسة الواحدة عن الارتباط الاخوي مع اخواتها الكنائس اردفتم ذلك بقولكم « كما وعن الكنائس الاميركية القائمة بمهام التبشير في هذه البلاد » وهذا يذكّرنا بخطاب تلاه أحدكم في مدرسة الاحد منذ بضع سنين وطبع في مطبعتكم جاء فيه « ان المجمع الذي ينفق على مدارسنا ومطابعنا الخ آلا يليق ان نخضع لنظاماته » فلا نعلم وجه العلاقة بين كنيسة مستقلة او اخرى يُطلب منها الاستقلال يؤدي اعضاؤها عن اولادهم الراتب المدرسي المعيّن واثمان الكتب كسائر الطوائف يحبّون ان يكون كتاب الله دستورهم الاول وبين الخضوع لانظمة يجهلونها كل الجهل وقد لا تلائم مصلحتهم ولا تنطبق على حاجة كنيستهم وبلادهم · والاعجب مما ذُكِر ان كاتم اسرار مجمعكم المرحوم الدكتور ميثبل عند وقوفه على بشرى استقلالنا قال لنا صراحةً في اجتماع حافل « أنا لا نطالبكم بجمع مشيخي قط ولا بخلافه بل عندكم كتاب الله وحده وما تسلّمتموه من المرسَلين الاولين فسير وا بموجب ذلك ونحن ندعو لكم بالبركة » وزد على ذلك ما نقلهُ لنا حديثًا

حضرة كاتب ارسالتكم عن لسان كاتم الاسرار الحالي ومؤدّاهُ كما مرّ
« انه بعد جولانهِ في الشرق واختبارهِ الكافي رأى ان النظام المشيخي
لا يلائم حال بلادنا وحاجتها » فاذا كان مجمعكم نفسهُ اعفانا من ممارسة هذا
النظام فما بال حضراتكم تدعوننا اليه وترغبون في إلباسنا اياهُ برُمّته بدون
تبديل ولا تعديل ؟

خامسًا. فلتم في لائحتكم بعد الكلام الآنف الذكر « وكل ذلك لاجل
الانضام الى كنيسة واحدة التي تأبى الارتباط بالنظام المشيخي ». وقد عجبنا
من هذا القول ايضًا. الا تستحق الكنيسة الواحدة ان تُراعى حرّيتها وضميرها ؟
الا يجدر بها المحافظة على سلامها ووحدتها وان يفضّل ذلك على كل ترتيب
بشري ؟ أتظنون ان تلك الانظمة موحى بها من الله ؟ أضرورية هي
للخلاص ؟ فقد عاش عدد وافر من الاتقياء كنيستنا العزيزة وماتوا على النظام
القديم أتظنون انهم هلكوا لعدم اتباعهم النظام الحديث ؟ فاين هذا من
قول الرسول « ان كان لحمًا يعثر اخي فلن آكل لحمًا الى الابد لئلا اعثر
اخي » وقولهُ « صرت لليهود كيهودي لاربح اليهود الخ » « من يضعف
وانا لا اضعف من يعثر وانا لا التهب » « لا يحكم احد في حرّيتكم »
« المسيح دعانا في الحرّية » « لا ترتبكوا بنير عبودية ». فاذا رمنا الاستناد
على نص الكتاب رأينا ان بنيان الكنيسة ووحدتها وائتلاف قلوب اعضائها
وتآزرهم في الروحيّات والاعال الخيرية امسّ واهمّ من كل نظام انسانيّ

سادسًا. انكم تحثّون الكنيستين على الانضام والاستقلال ثم تطلبون
منهما الخضوع للنظام المشيخي كل الخضوع. فاذا قمنا باستقلالنا واغنيناكم عن
انفاق النفقات والاهتمام بامورنا أليس لنا والحالة هذه الحق بان نبقى ثابتين
على النظام الذي وُلدنا فيه ورضعناه مع اللبن ؟ الا ترون ان النظام المشيخي
نفسهُ تختلف به بعض الكنائس عن الاخرى ؟ فكنائس دمشق واللاذقية
ومصر التي نوّهتم بذكرها في لائحتكم تختلف عن كنائس مجمعكم بعض

الاختلاف · وكذلك كنائس سكوتلاندا عن امركا وفرنسا عنهـا في بعض الامور · وقد قال لنا حضرة كاتب ارسالیتكم « ان المجمع الذي تأسس في سوريا ليس هو الأ رسم لا حقيقة وانه° متى استقلّت كنيستان او ثلث تسن لنفسها النظام الذي تريده°.... فما بالكم من جهة تعترضون على الاستقلال ومن جهة تعارضوننا به وتريدون ان نخضع خضوعًا تامًا لانظمة لا يزال اهمها في حيز الكتمان ؟

سابعًا · فقلنا « ان كنيستنا لم تمتحن فعليًا النظام المشيخي ولم تفسد صحته° بـبراهين انجيلية او عقلية » فيا ترى أ أفسدتم حضرتكم اولاً نظامنا القديم المحافظين عليه° والمسنون من سائتكم الافاضل بـبراهين انجيلية وعقلية ام ابطلتم صحته° بالبينات الدامغة ؟ ام يا ترى أ أثبتم نظامكم المشيخي بالبراهين المذكورة ؟ ام هل دفعتروها لنا لنطالعها فنقتنع ؟ ام كيف يمكننا افساد ما نجهل تفاصيله° ودقائقه° المجموعة عندكم في مجلد ضخم او مجلدات ؟ فكان الاولى ان تترجموا الكتاب المذكور او اهمه° وتنشروه° مطبوعًا وتكرموا علينا بزمان كافٍ لمطالعته° · وحينئذٍ تدعون من استحسن تلك الانظمة للانتظام في سلكها وتعطون من أبى قبولها ورام البقاء على النظام القديم حريةً باتباع اقتناع ضميره° · فتكونون قد اجريتم العدل ودرأتم كل مشكل ونزاع · أما فتشنا الانجيل بأسره° فلم نعثر على ذكر انعقاد مجامع سنوية اقليمية ومجامع سينودس اعلى ومجامع عامة مسكونية اعلى منها ولم نرَ تلميحًا لشيء من ذلك سوى التئام الرسل والشيوخ في اورشليم للنظر في قضية دينية ازعجت كنيسة انطاكية لوقوع الخلاف بين المؤمنين من اليهود والامم في مسألة الختان · فبعثت تلك الكنيسة بولس وبرنابا الى اورشليم لاستفتاء الرسل وشيوخ الكنيسة في الامر · فحكموا بإلهام الروح باعفاء المؤمنين من هذا الفرض الذي ابطله° المسيح مع سائر الفروض الطقسية · وكان للرسل وحدهم حق الحكم بالمسألة بالنظر لما أعطوه° من الوحي والسلطة الروحية الرسولية ·

ولم يجمعوا معهم اعمدة كنيسة قيصرية و يافا واللد ودمشق وغيرها ۰ وهذا هو المجمع الوحيد الذي يصرح به سفر الاعمال ۰ ولم يذكر بعدئذٍ التئام كنائس فلسطين ولا اسيا الصغرى ولا اليونان او مكدونية وغيرها ۰ ولم يضع المسيح ولا الرسل امرًا بالتئام مجامع سنوية لسنّ انظمة و فروض تضغط على الكنائس وتضع عليها اثقالاً قد تكون فوق احتمالها ۰ فلا نعلم على اي امرٍ الهي او رسولي بنيتم هذا المجمع الاّ اذا كنتم بنيتموه على المجمع اليهودي السبعيني (الذي حكم على مخلصنا بالصلب) كما اشرتم الى ذلك صريحًا في احد اعداد النشرات الاسبوعية منذ نحو سنتين ۰ (وهنا بحث طويل لا نحب الخوض فيه الان وعندنا بشأنه كلام كثير نرجئه الى ما بعد الوقوف على ابواب تلك الانظمة وفصولها المسهبة)

ثامنًا ۰ في اثناء ابحاثنا ومناقشاتنا المديدة بهذه المسألة التي دامت اعوامًا سألناكم عن الغايات التي دعتكم الى عقد هذا المجمع تفصيلاً فعددتموها لنا واحدة فواحدة فرقناها كلها وقبلناها بعد التعديل حبًا بالسلام وضنًا بوحدة الكنيسة وراحتها ۰ ووقعها اعضاء الكنيسة كلهم بعد اخذ الصوت القانوني بشأنها واجماع الاراء ۰ ثم وقعها حضرة كاتب ارساليتكم الفاضل ۰ ثم ضربتم صفحًا عن تلك اللائحة وجئتم الان تطالبونا بالنظام المشيخي برمته ۰ فاذا كانت تلك الغايات التي ذكرتموها وقبلناها وقتئذٍ هي وحدها النظام المشيخي فلماذا اودعتموها زوايا النسيان ؟ واذا كانت غيرها لماذا لم تقيدونا عنها حينئذٍ ؟ وقد قال جناب كاتب ارساليتكم في الجلسة التي الفها حديثًا للمذاكرة بمسألة الانضمام ان اللائحة المذكورة لا تختلف عن النظام المشيخي الا بامرٍ واحد ۰ وهو ان النظام المذكور من قوانينه التئام المجمع كل سنة اما اللائحة فحين الاقتضاء ۰۰ فيا تُرى اذا لم يكن للمجمع شغل مهم ينظر فيه فما هو الباعث على تعطيل اوقات قسوس الكنائس ونوابها وتجشم مشقات السفر ونفقاته وتحمُّل الاثقال والتعرُّض

لاخطار الحرّ والبرد والركوب في بعض الطرق الوعرة الخ ؟ فاذا حضر
اولئك النواب ولم يكن عندهم مشاكل يُطلَب منهم فضّها والحكم بها ولا
مسائل للمذاكرة بشأنها الا يكون اجتماعهم باعثًا بالاحرى على فتح ابواب
لاقاويل ومناقشات وسنّ قوانين جديدة نحن في غنى عنها ؟ وربما ادّى
الامر الى مطاعن وانتقادات تدعونا الواجبات المسيحية لـسدّ ابوابها٠ الا
يخوّلنا نظامنا القديم الحق عند وقوع مشاكل في كنيسة تعجز عمدتها عن
حلّها ان تدعو تلك الكنيسة قسوس الكنائس اخواتها ونوّابها لاسعافها
والاشتراك معها بحسمها ؟ فلماذا نحمّل انفسنا نحن الضعفاء القليلي العدد
اثقالاً ونفقات تأنّ منها كنائس امركا المشيخية الغنية نفسها ؟ كما انبأ أنا
كاتب ارساليتكم الفاضل المحبوب الراغب كل الرغبة في انضمامنا

تاسعًا٠ قلتم « انه بناءً على وجود النظام المشيخي في الابرشيات التي هي
تحت ادارتكم ليس لكم بعد ان تحكموا بالمسائل المتعلقة بالنظام الكنسي بل
يتوجب عليكم احالة كل هذه المسائل الى المجمع المشيخي لاجل التبصّر
والحكم بها » ونحن نرى ان هذا الامر بيدكم ويُناط بارادتكم٠ لان هذه
الكنائس لا تعلم شيئًا عن هذا النظام الذي وضعتموه عليها وضغطتم به
على حرّيتها كما انّا لا نعلمهُ نحن٠ولو سُئل احد اعضائها عمّا يعلمونهُ عن
هذا النظام لاجابوا انهم لا يعلمون عنهُ شيئًا سوى تعيين الثمامه في البلدة
الفلانية٠ولو سئلوا عن المواضيع والابحاث التي تجري فيه لاجابوا انّى لنا
الالمام بما لم نُخبَرعنهُ٠ بل لو سألتَ اكثر اعضائه انفسهم لاجابوا بمثل
ذلك٠وقد عجبنا من قولكم ان تلك الابرشيات هي تحت ادارتكم ثم تقولون
ليس لكم ان تحكموا بالمسائل٠ أليس لكم الصوت الاقوى في احكامهِ ؟ومن
الغريب انكم من اشدّ اعضائهِ نفوذًا وتحكمون على من اخطأ من سائر
اعضائه وغيرهم ولايُحكم على من اخطأ من سائر اعضاءارساليتكم الامر
المنافي لسنن سائر المجالس والمحاكم والمغاير العدالة والانصاف ٠ والخلاصة

أنا نعتقد انكم لو شئتم لضممتم الكنيستين في يوم واحد ٠ اذ لا يوجد بين
اعضائها لله الحمد عدوان شخصي ولاضغائن ولا منافرات توجب الانفصال
والابتعاد ٠ ونحن نعتبر اخوتنا من الكنيسة الاخرى ونعزهم ٠ والاكثرون
منهم اذا لم نقل الجميع يصبون الى الانضمام ويتوقون اليه نظيرنا بملء
القلوب لانهم م نظيرنا رضعوه مع اللبن ٠ فلماذا تبعدوننا عن ميراثنا ونصيبنا
في اسرائيل ونحرمونا من لذة الائتلاف الروحي الاخوي وفوائده ؟ ونحن
شرذمة صغيرة ضعيفة ضحت كلا عزّ وهان واحتملت التعيير والذل حبّا
بانجيل مخلصها العزيز ٠ ! اما كفانا الانفراد عن الاهل والاعزّاء ؟ اما كفانا
تنكيت الخارجين عن طائفتنا وانتقادهم ؟ اما كفانا حرماننا من اعزّ
حقوقنا المدنية ؟ حتى نجعل انقسامنا ضغثًا على ابّالة ؟ ألستم انتم دُعاة
انجيل السلام ومرسلي اله المحبة وخدّام من بذل حياته لجمع شتات
اسرائيل والام ؟ فان كنا لا نرجو منكم المسالمة والمصالحة حسب ارادة من
صالحنا بدم صليبه فممّن ؟

عاشرًا ٠ فلتم تحت البند الاول من نصائحكم « انه يتوجب على كل
كنيسة ان تقوم بكامل مصروفها بنفسها بقدر ما يمكنها وباوّل ما يمكنها
ذلك وان تبذل قصارى الجهد في الوصول الى هذا المقصود ولو افضى الامر
الى انكار الذات الكلي من اعضائها افرادًا واجمالاً » فنقول انا بمعونة الله
وبركته قد قمنا بهذا الامر واغنيناكم عن ازعاج انفسكم بزيادة الحثّ
والحضّ ٠ وكما حمدًا لله باكورة كنائس سوريا القائمة بهذه الواجبة ونرجو
ان نرى سائر كنائسنا المحبوبة تسعى نحو هذا الغرض تدريجًا فيزداد
سرورنا و يشتدّ ازرنا باستقلالها ٠ على انا نشكر كم كثيرًا لاجل هذا التنبيه
ونسأله تعالى ان بأخذ يدنا في تحقيقه الى النهاية

حادي عشر ٠ جاء في لائحتكم في البند الثاني « انه يتوجب على كل
كنيسة ان تحافظ بكل غيرة ودقة على مبدإ الاعتماد على الحكم باكثرية

الاصوات في ادارة شو ُونها · لكون هذا المبدأ من اركان الحرية والانصاف في الكنيسة · · نعم هذا مبدأ طبيعي في سائر الاعمال القانونية · وهذا ما جرينا عليه منذ البداءة ولا نزال محافظين عليه كل المحافظة · غير ان الاعتماد على اصوات اعضاء الكنيسة الغرباء الذين إقامتهم بيننا موقتة ولا يعلمون احوال الكنيسة وحاجتها الحقيقية كل العلم ولا يهمهم امرها كما يهم أعضاءها المتوطنين · وكذلك الاعتماد على الاعضاء الذين لا يؤدون شيئًا لخدمة المنبر وسائر نفقات الكنيسة وتلامذة المدارس كل ذلك مسألة تستدعي البحث ودقة النظر والتعاون على حلها بوجه عادل لا يجحف بمصلحة الكنيسة وبخيرها الحقيقيين · وقد عجبنا من قولكم انه يتوجب على كل كنيسة ان تحافظ على مبدأ الاعتماد على الحكم باكثرية الاصوات في ادارة شو ُونها وانكم بعد تأملات كثيرة الخ · زاد يقينكم ان النظام المشيخي هو ابسط ما يكون في المارسة الخ · فيا ُترى مع بَن من الكنائس اجر يتم المخابرة بشأن هذا النظام ؟ وهل اخذتم صوت الكنيسة هنا المؤلفة من اكثر من ١٠٠ صوت ؟ وهل اخذتم اصوات سائر الكنائس قانونيًا بهذا الموضوع · فكيف تحثوننا على الجري بحسب اكثرية الاصوات وانتم لا تسير ون على ذلك · والظاهر انكم اخذتم اصوات اعضاء ارساليتكم فقط (اصوات المرسلين) واهملتم سائر الكنائس · أيحسب هذا من باب العدالة ؟

ثاني عشر · ورد في لائحتكم تحت البند الثالث « انه يتوجب على كل كنيسة ان تحفظ بيدها ادارة ماليتها ولا يسوغ لها مطلقًا تسليم هذه الادارة لبد وكلاء او لجنة او جمعية ولو من اعضائها القانونيين ان لم يكن هولاء قد أقيموا لذلك باقتخابها الحر وقابلين للتجديد والتنزيل والتبديل باصواتها هي ومكلفين بتقديم كل نقريراتهم لها لاجل المصادقة ومسؤولين عما في كل شيء بعد مسؤوليتهم لله » فهذا ما قد جرينا عليه ايضًا وننوي التمسك به اننا يستثنى من ذلك العقار والمال الموقوف الذي تتصرف به جمعية

الكنيسة بحسب ارادة الواقف ٠ فاذا وضع الواقف العناية بموقوفه تحت ادارة الجمعية الخيرية لاسواها لايحق لما ان تحوّل هذه العناية الى غيرها بل يفرض عليها شرعًا ان تواصل العناية بما أُودع في يدها وتنفقه في السبيل الذي عيّنه الواقف لاغير

ثالث عشر ٠ قلتم ايضًا في البند الرابع من لائحتكم «انه يتوجب على كل كنيسة الانضمام الى سائر الكنائس المخاوية لها بالايمان والمجاورة لما والارتباط النظامي الاشدّ ما يمكن معها ٠ اولاً لاجل صيانتها ٠ ثم لزيادة التحسين والتأثير في خدمتها الخارجية ٠٠ وعلى ذلك نجيب ٠ اننا كما منضمين مع سائر الكنائس المخاوية لنا بالايمان مدةً لاتقل عن ٤٨ سنة تحت نظام واحد بسيط سنه المرسلون الأولون الافاضل ولم يحدث بيننا وبينها لله الحمد خلاف ولا انقسام وكانا ميايرين واياها على اتم المصافاة ونجاح وسرور ولم تنشا مشاكل ضمنها تستوجب الحل ٠٠ ولم يحدث فيها انحراف عن العقائد التي تسلمناها واقررنا بها بعهد مقدس عند دخولنا في شركة الكنيسة الانجيلية ٠ ونحب بمل٠ قلوبنا المحافظة على عبودنا الرهيبة ونودّ ان لاتلم وتنكث بعهود اخرى ٠ ولايظن أنا معارضون لكل نظام بل نرى من الواجبات المقدسة التمسك بالنظام المتفق عليه صيانة للكنيسة من تطرّق الخلل اليها وحرصًا على وحدتنا وارتباطنا ولزيادة التحسين والتأثير في خدمتها الخارجية كما المعتم الى ذلك ٠ ولا نحب فقط الاتصال عن سائر الكنائس اخواتنا بل نحسب الانفصال افة كبرى يجب دفعها بكل الوسائل الممكنة ٠ ونحن نترحب بكل عضو يشرّفنا بزيارته من تلك الكنائس ٠ ونودّ ان نبسط لبعضايد التآزر والتعاضد ونتبادل معًا الاراء الآيلة لخير الكنيسة وترقيتها

رابع عشر ٠ جاء ايضًا في رسالتكم «انه مع محافظتكم على حرية الكنائس في ادارة شؤونها لايخطر لكم على بال ان تحكموا فيها وانكم تحسبون ان علاقاتكم معها كثيرة ومهمة وشديدة وتعتبرون صالحها ونموّها من اعز

الامور عندكم. ولذلك تصرحون لما انكم بعد تأملات كثيرة ومخابرات مستوفية واختبارات متسعة قد زاد يقينكم بان النظام المشيخي الجاري الان في الكنائس السورية الانجيلية اجمالاً هو ابسط في المارسة واسلم ما يكون من الاخطار وافعل ما يكون في خدمة هذا الصالح وهذا النور» وهنا كنا نود ان نضبط القلم عن الاستفاضة بهذا البحث والمناقشة بشأنه. لانا لسنا في موقف جدال ولا اننا كما سبق ان قلنا لا نستطيع الرد تفصيلاً على نظام نجهل اكثره، وهو موضوع في صفحات مجلد ضخم عجز مجمعكم نفسه عن تلخيصه واختصاره. وان قيل ان النظام المشيخي مترجم ومطبوع فنجيب ان هذا الكراس الصغير ليس الأ رسم لاحقيقة كما قال احدكم. وان ما تُرجم منه قليل جداً وما لا يعتد به بالنسبة. وقد عجبنا من قولكم انه ابسط ما يكون مع انه كثير التراكيب والابواب والفصول الطوال و يستلزم الدرس الدقيق وتخصيص قسم كبير من الزمان لاستيعابه. ونحن بسرور نخبركم ان نظامنا الذي سرنا عليه منذ نشأة الكنيسة في سورية لم نرَ فيه عيباً ولذلك نسير عليه الى ما شاء الله. واما قولكم انه اسلم ما يكون من الاخطار وافعل ما يكون في خدمة هذا الصالح فهذا لم تثبتوه ببينة عملية. ولم نرَ ان الكنائس استفادت منه في روحياتها ومادياتها. بل لم تخلُ اجتماعاته من اختلاف الاراء والاقاويل والتشويش والنزاع كما حدث في ميناره (بحقل طرابلس) وزحلة وحاصبيا والجديدة وصيدا. حتى ان المجمع الذي التأم في العام الغابر بايرشية صيدا لم تحضر اليه ثلاث كنائس مهمة في الحقل المذكور ولم تكن تلك الكنائس ممثلة في جلساته. وما ادرانا بما ينجم عن هذه الاجتماعات السنوية من زيادة الخلاف في الاستقبال الامر الذي نحاذر كل المحاذرة من الوقوع فيه. وفضلاً عما ذُكر لم تبرهنوا لنا كون نظامنا خطراً وضعيف الفعل والتأثير. اما واقعة الحال فتبرهن عكس ما المتم به

واسمحوا لنا ان نقول في معرض الكلام عن « النظام المشيخي » ان
كلمة « مشيخة » التي تنسبونها الى هذا النظام مأخوذة من ١ تي ٤ : ٨ في
قول الرسول تيموثاوس « لا تهمل الموهبة التي فيك المعطاة لك بالنبوة
ووضع ايدي المشيخة » اي القسوس او رعاة الكنائس او المتقدمين بالسن
والاختبار الروحي من خُدّامها . فهؤلاء لم يضعوا للكنائس نظاماً مكتوباً
ولا فرضوا عليها الاجتماع سنوياً في مجامع اقليمية او عامةً . وقد عجبنا من
انكم اضفتم رتبةً رابعةً الى الكنيسة وهي الشيوخ المدبرون الذين تعتبرونهم
بمنزلة قسوس وترسمونهم في وظيفة دائمة . على ان الرسول حين كتب
لكنيسة فيلبي قال « الى اساقفة (او قسوس كما في حاشية التوراة) وشمامسة
ومؤمنين » فلو وُجدت درجة رابعة لما تغاضى عن ذكرها . واذا اجتمع
الا يقول الرسول « اما الشيوخ المدبرون حسناً فليُحسبوا اهلاً لكرامة
مضاعفة » نجيب ان كلمة مدبرين هي صفة للشيوخ او القسوس الممتازين
بالتقدُّم في السنّ والاختبار . لا وظيفة كنسية خاصةً . ولا يخفى ان
للبعض في الكنيسة موهبة التدبير كوجود موهبة التعليم والترجمة وغيرها .
فلا نقول ان كل الذين يمتازون بهذه المواهب يكونون من طغمة القسوس
الاّ اذا حملتم هذا التعليم على الاستحسان . فاذا فتحنا باباً لما نستحسنه نحن
لا الكتاب يخشى ان يؤدي بنا الامر الى ١٠لا تحمد عقباه . ثم اذا كان
الشيوخ هم برتبة القسوس وغير قابلين العزل والابدال كما هي الحال في المجمع
المشيخي كان اعضاء المجمع كلّهم من رتبة الاكليروس والشعب غير ممثل
فيه .١٠اذ لا يحضره سوى قسوس وشيوخ . وعلى ذلك كانت الكنيسة محرومة
من حرية انتخاب نوابها . اما سبب هذا الشقاق فيكون القسيس والنائب
فقط لا الكنيسة . وقد قلتم انه لا يخطر على بالكم قط ان تحكموا في الكنائس
فاذا كنتم لا تحكمون لماذا لا تتركون لكنيستينا الانجيليتين في بيروت
حرية الانضمام ؟ بل لماذا لا تحضُّونا عليه ونسعفونا على تحقيقه كما هو

المرجو من رعاة يعتبرون صالح الكنيسة ونموها من أعزّ الامور عندهم كما
نوّهتم بذلك في رسالتكم . فأنتم اصحاب النفوذ الاول في الكنائس ولا نظن
انها تعارضكم اذا رغبتم في التوفيق بين الكنيستين بل الجميع يساعدونكم
على ذلك

خامس عشر . قلتم ايضًا « بما ان احدى الكنيستين الانجيليتين في
بيروت هي الان متحدة مع الكنائس الاخرى في النظام المشيخي فالامر
غنيٌّ عن البيان انه ليس بعد من خصائصكم حلّها من هذا الارتباط . كما
وانها هي لا تقدر ان تفسخ هذه العلاقة ولا ان تقوم بمشروع مهمّ مستقلة
بدون استشارة المجمع المشيخي الاوتكون قد مسّت ناموس الكنائس اخواتها
وواجباتها وعهودها الناجمة عن علاقاتها المشيخية . وانه يُعَدّ من اعظم
فوائد النظام المشيخي وقاية كل كنيسة مرتبطة بهذا النظام من الوقوع في
تغييرات عجولة او مغايرة للحكمة والعدالة » . وعلى ذلك نجيب . ان
ارتباط اعضاء كنيسة واحدة مع بعضهم اهمّ من ارتباط تلك الكنيسة مع
كنائس اخرى . فاللتان تسمّونهما كنيسي بيروت الانجيليتين هما بالحقيقة
كنيسة واحدة . ويسوؤنا ان نسمع كونهما كنيستين . نعم قد انفصل
القسم الواحد عن الاخر لاسباب لم يكن منشاؤها اعضاء الكنيسة انقسمهم .
لكنّا لم نيأس بعد من الانضمام . فاعضاء القسمين كانوا متحدين معًا
مدّةً لا تقلّ عن ٥٠ سنة . ونظن ان اتحادهما الديني والاخوي والطبيعي
يجب ان يُعتبر امتن من اتحاد القسم الواحد مع المجمع المشيخي منذ نحو
سنتين فقط . على ان ذلك الاتحاد لا يشمل سائر الاعضاء الذين قلّما
عرفوا شيئًا عن هذا الاتحاد ونظامه وشروطه . ولم يمثّل الكنيسة فيه سوى
قسيس واحد ونائب واحد . فكان الأولى ان تضموا القسمين اولًا ليقوما
بالاستقلال الذي ترغبون فيه وتحرّضون عليه وتحسبونه ويحسبه جميعكم
في امركا امرًا اوّليًا . ثم تعرضوا عليهما النظام الجديد بعد بيانه الكافي

١٩

وتركوا لها الحرية بقبوله او تعديله او البقاء على القديم حسبا يتفقان ٠
ولا سيما لان مجمعكم الامريكي نفسهُ يشير بذلك ويوصي بهِ ٠ كما تبيّن لنا
من كاتبي اسرارهِ الفاضلَين المرحوم الدكتور ميتشل والسكرتر الحالي
الموصوف بالحكمة والفطنة والاخبار ٠ واما قولكم ليس من خصائصكم حلُّ
الكنيسة اخذنا من هذا الارتباط فقد اجبنا عنهُ فيا سبق ولا نطلب منكم
حلَّها بل ان تتركوا لها حرية العمل والاتفاق معنا ٠ونظن ان اكثر الاخوة
في الكنيسة الاخرى اذا لم نقل كلهم لوتُرِكت لهم حرية الارادة لفضّلوا
الانضام وآثروهُ ٠ اذ لا توجد ينهم وبيننا اسباب شخصية توجب
الانفصال والابتعاد ٠ولم يروا في نظامهم السابق ما يوجب تركهُ والانضام
الى النظام المشيخي ٠واما قولكم « ان الكنيسـة اختنا لا نقدر ان تفسخ هذه
العلاقة ولا ان نقوم بمشروع مهم مستقلّة بدون استشارة المجمع المشيخي
الاّ وتكون قد مسّت ناموس الكنائس اخواتها وواجباتها وعهودها الناجمة
عن علاقاتها المشيخية » الخ ٠ فهذا قد استغربناه كل الاستغراب ٠
ألا يسوغ لكنيسة القيام بمشروع مهم بدون ان تكون مقسورة على استشارة
سائر الكنائس التي ربما لا تستحسن ذلك المشروع الذي ايقن اعضاء تلك
الكنيسـة انهُ نافع مهم ؟ فاين الحرية التي دعانا بها المسيح ؟ فقد غللتم
ايدي الكنائس عن العناية بنفسها والسعي وراء مصلحتها ٠ فلو فُرض
انعقاد المجمع المشيخي في نيسان وفي ايار عنّ لاعضاء كنيسة القيام بمشروع
مفيد أتوّجل الامر احد عشر شهرًا الى ان يلتئم المجمع وتستشيرهُ عند
فوات الفرصة الملائمة ؟ وفي حال كهذه نقرّ لحضراتكم ان هذا النظام بدلاً
من ان يكون جاذبًا اسمى دافعًا يدفعنا عن التقيد بسلاسل يتعذّر علينا
احتمالها ٠ ولا نظن ان اخوتنا في الكنيسة الاخرى علموا بهذا القيد وتمهدوا
به ٠ وعلى كل نرى ان لم ولنا الحرية باختيار ما نراهُ معًا ملائمًا لخير
كنيستنا ومصلحتها ٠ ولمّا كنتم انتم ممثلي حرّية الافكار الروحية لا نظن

انكم تشجعوننا على خسارتها وفقدها

سادس عشر . جاء في ختام لائحتكم ما نصهُ «انكم تُسرّون بان العناية الالهيّة سهّلت السبيل لحل هذه المسألة في وقت غير بعيد وبطريقة جميلة بواسطة الاجتماع المشيخي المعيّن التئامهُ في بيروت في نيسان القادم لان هذا المجمع هو الوارث القانوني لكافة الحقوق والمسؤولية التي كانت لكم وعليكم في ادارة الاحكام والنظامات الكنسية وهذه الوراثة مؤيدة ليس فقط بتقريرات ارساليتكم الرسمية بل ايضاً بموجب النظام القديم الذي تأسست عليه الكنائس الانجيلية في هذه البلاد » امّا نحن فنظن ان العناية الالهية تسهّل كل حين المسألة والاتحاد متى وُجِدت الارادة المخلصة وأُزيلت الموانع . ولا نظن ان اخوتنا اعضاء المجمع يجوّزون انفصال كنيستنا . لان ما نشهدهُ فيهم من الحبّ المسيحي والغيرة يوطد رجاءنا بحسن نياتهم نحونا . وقد قلتم «ان هذه الوراثة مؤيدة ليس فقط بتقريرات ارساليتكم الرسمية بل بموجب بنود النظام القديم الذي تأسست عليه الكنائس الانجيلية في هذه البلاد » فقد سررنا من قولكم هذا ونحب ان نذعن لما نؤمنم به . فانكم قلتم « ان النظام القديم تأسست عليه الكنائس الانجيلية في هذه البلاد » والنظام المذكور يقول « اذا وُجد في كنيسة مشكل عجزت عمدة تلك الكنيسة عن حله يُدعى قسوس الكنائس ونوّابها لاسعاف تلك الكنيسة على حله » ولا نظن ان كنيستنا عجزت بعد عن فض هذا الاشكال . لانها لم تلتئم قانونياً بعد للنظر فيه . فقد التأمت مرّة ومرّتين وتباحثت مليا في المسألة وابدت عجزها . حينئذ تدعو هي قسوس الكنائس ونوّابها لاسعافها . ولما كانت كنائسنا حسب قولكم تأسست على هذا النظام فنحب ان نرسخ عليه ولا نريد تغييرهُ وفقاً لاقتناع ضمائرنا . ولئلا نكون عرضة للمنتقدين من سائر الطوائف

ولا تظنّوا أنا عرضنا هذه الأمور لديكم بكذاخر يةووضوح لاغراض في
النفس ، معاذ الله ، ولا يخطر لنا يال ان نبخسكم حقكم من الا كرام والتجلة
فأنّا مقدّرون اعمالكم التبشيرية والخيرية والعلمية حق قدرها ولا نقابلها الاّ
باسداء الشكر الجزيل والثناء لكم ولمجمعكم الاميركي الموقّر ، واختلافنا
على النظام لا يؤثّر باتحادنا في مبادىٔ كتاب الله العزيز الجوهرية ، ولا
بالعواطف والمقاصد لاجل البنيان والنموّ في الروحيات ونشر كلمة الحياة في
وطننا المحبوب ، أنختلف على الكساء ونغادر الجسم الحي يتألم ويهزل ،
فاذا اختلف شريكي عني بالثوب والزيّ لا ارى هذا الاختلاف حاملاً
على مجافاته وقطع علائقي الودّية معه ، وعندنا انهٔ اذا تعذّر من سوء
الحظ انضمام الكنيستين في مكان عبادة واحد لا يتعذر بيركة الله انضمام
القلوب في الحبّ المسيحي والمحافظة على العلائق الاخوية ، أنا نرى في
هذه الايام الكنائس الانجيلية في امركا وانكلترا وغيرها تبذل قصارى
الجهد في التقارب والمصافاة وعقد لجان ومؤتمرات من قسومها واعضائها
لاقامة الاجتماعات الروحيةوالمباحثات بصالح الكنيسة العام والبشارة وبكلا
يؤدّي الى ترقية مصالح الانجيل والاتحاد فلماذا لا نكون نحن كذلك ؟
فأنا جميعاًون؟ من ائنأواحداً ونقول بحقائق انجيلية واحدة ولنا رجاءواحد ،
ةلا يقل احدنا انا لبولس واخر انا لابلّس واخرانا لصفا » لاتنا جميعاً جسد
المسيح واعضاؤهٔ افراداً » ولم نتجرأ على مخاطبتكم!ٕ اعرضناهٔ الاّ لكي نكشف
قلوبنا لكم كا لرعاة غيورين افاضل يهمّهم نمّ الكنيسة وسلامها ووحدتها
وقد بذلوا جهد المستطاع في غرس الحق الالهي في حديقتها وتربيتها
وتغذيتها الى ان شبّت على المبادىٔ الانجيلية الصافية التي نرغب كل الرغبة
في المحافظة عليها ، ولا نظن انهٔ يهون عليكم تمزيق الكنيسة وتثنيتها،
فنكم نرجو اسعافنا على مواساة الكلوم ورتق الصدع وتأليف القلوب

وفي الختام نستغيث برئيس كنيستنا الالهي ان يلهمنا جميعًا الى ما به
السلام والائتلاف ويرينا السبيل القويم والوسيلة الفضلى لحلّ هذا
المشكل وإزالة كل خلاف وعثرة من سبيل لتقدم ملكوته ونمو كنيسته .
كما انّا نستغيث ايضًا بغيرة اخوتنا واخواتنا الاعزاء في كنيستنا
الواحدة الانجيلية ببيروت (ولا نقول الكنيسة الاخرى)
وسائر كنائس سوريا الانجيلية ونستنجد بحميتهم وشهامتهم
ومحبتهم المسيحية وزجوم المؤازرة بالادعية والاراء
وبذل الهمّة لنوال الوحدة الاخوية التي نصبو
اليها جميعًا تحت ادارة رئيسنا الالهي
وتأثير روح القدوس .

امين

بأمر الكنيسة الانجيلية
الوطنية وعمدتها
نعوم ثابت
(شماس)